# Contents

# EGG SALAD ALGIERS

**Prep Time:** 15 mins

**Total Time:** 15 mins

**Servings per Recipe:** 8

**NUTRITIONAL VALUE**

Calories 109.8 ,Fat 6.6g ,Cholesterol 56.8mg ,Sodium 132.5mg ,Carbohydrates 4.3g ,Protein 8.5g

**INGREDIENTS**

- 2 tsps red wine vinegar

- 2 tbsps olive oil

- 3 tomatoes, diced

- 3 mint leaves, sliced

- salt and pepper

- 1/2 tsp harissa

- 1 (6 oz.) cans tuna in vegetable oil

- 1 bell pepper, seeded and diced

- 2 hard-boiled eggs, peeled and sliced

- 1/2 small fennel bulb, diced

- 1 tbsp capers

- 1/2 red onion, peeled and diced

- black olives

**DIRECTIONS**

**Step 1**

Get a large mixing bowl: Whisk in it the vinegar, olive oil, mint, and harissa.

**Step 2**

Mix in the pepper, fennel, onion, tomato, a pinch of salt and pepper. Spoon the mixture into a serving plate.

**Step 3**

Arrange over it the sliced eggs, olives, tuna and capers. Serve your salad immediately.

**Step 4**

Enjoy.

# MY FIRST COUSCOUS

**Prep Time:** 20 mins

**Total Time:** 1 hr 50 mins

**Servings per Recipe:** 3

**NUTRITIONAL VALUE**

Calories 873.4 ,Fat 12.3g ,Cholesterol 0.0mg ,Sodium 629.2mg ,Carbohydrates 165.1g ,Protein 28.0g

**INGREDIENTS**

- 2 C. uncooked couscous
- 1 tbsp chili paste
- 2 tbsps olive oil
- 1/2 tbsp paprika
- 1 large onion, cubed
- 1/2 tbsp cinnamon
- 1 large green pepper, cubed
- 1/2 tbsp cumin

- 1 large zucchini, cubed

- 1 tsp salt and pepper

- 2 potatoes

- 2 carrots

- 14 oz. chickpeas

- 4 tbsps tomato paste

**DIRECTIONS**

**Step 1**

Place a large saucepan over medium heat. Heat in it the oil.

**Step 2**

Cook in it the onion for 3 min. Stir in the tomato paste, chickpeas, and 1 C. of water.

**Step 3**

Bring them to a rolling boil for 16 min. Stir in the veggies with 4 1/4 C. of water.

**Step 4**

Cook them until they start boiling. Let them cook for 40 to 46 min over low heat.

**Step 5**

Get large bowl: Pour over it 1 C. of boiling water with 1 C. of sauce from the stew.

**Step 6**

Let it sit for 6 min. Strain the couscous from excess liquid. Transfer it to a serving bowl.

**Step 7**

Spoon the veggies stew over it then serve it warm.

**Step 8**

Enjoy.

# GARLICKY LAMB

**Prep Time:** 15 mins

**Total Time:** 50 mins

**Servings per Recipe:** 4

**NUTRITIONAL VALUE**

Calories 382.7 ,Fat 17.2g ,Cholesterol 741.9mg ,Sodium 427.9mg ,Carbohydrates 13.8g ,Protein 42.3g

**INGREDIENTS**

- 28 oz. fresh lamb liver, 1 inch wide pieces

- 6-8 garlic cloves, minced

- salt & freshly ground black pepper

- 2 C. chopped tinned tomatoes with juice

- 1 C. water

- 1/2 C. chopped fresh coriander

- 2 tbsp. good quality olive oil

- 2-3 tsp. fresh ground cumin

**DIRECTIONS**

**Step 1**

Place a large pan over medium heat. Heat in it the oil.

**Step 2**

Cook in it the liver pieces for 2 to 3 min on each side.

**Step 3**

Lower the heat and let them cook for an extra 6 min. Stir in the garlic with cumin.

**Step 4**

Cook them for 1 min while stirring. Stir in the tomato with a pinch of salt and pepper.

**Step 5**

Cook them for 2 min. Stir in the water and put on the lid. Cook them for 26 min.

**Step 6**

Once the time is up, add the coriander.

**Step 7**

Adjust the seasoning of your liver stew then serve it hot with some rice.

**Step 8**

Enjoy.

# FATHIA'S BEAN BOWLS

**Prep Time:** 15 mins

**Total Time:** 2 hr 30 mins

**Servings per Recipe:** 4

**NUTRITIONAL VALUE**

Calories 832.3 ,Fat 43.3g ,Cholesterol 187.2mg ,Sodium 366.6mg ,Carbohydrates 46.6g ,Protein 63.3g

**INGREDIENTS**

- 1 C. dried lima beans, soaked overnight

- chopped

- and drained

- 2 C. chicken stock

- 2 tbsp. olive oil

- 4 C. water

- 26.5 oz. lamb

- 14 oz. chopped tomatoes

- 2 medium brown onions, coarsely

- 4 tbsp. chopped fresh coriander

- chopped

- 2 tbsp. lemon juice

- 2 garlic cloves, crushed

- 2 medium carrots, coarsely chopped

- 2 celery ribs, trimmed and coarsely

**DIRECTIONS**

**Step 1**

Place a pot over medium heat. Heat in it the oil.

**Step 2**

Cook in it the lamb pieces for 2 min on each side.

**Step 3**

Stir in the veggies and cook them for 4 min. Stir in the stock with water and beans.

**Step 4**

Heat them until they start boiling. Lower the heat and put on the lid.

**Step 5**

Cook them for 60 min while discarding the rising foam on top every 30 min.

**Step 6**

Once the time is up, drain the lamb pieces and shred them.

**Step 7**

Stir them back into the pot with tomatoes. Put on the lid and cook them for an extra 60 min.

**Step 8**

Turn off the heat and add the lemon juice with coriander.

**Step 9**

Adjust the seasoning of your soup then serve it hot.

**Step 10**

Enjoy.

# ALGERIAN CREPES

**Prep Time:** 10 mins

**Total Time:** 40 mins

**Servings per Recipe:** 6

**NUTRITIONAL VALUE**

Calories 444.7 ,Fat 6.8g ,Cholesterol 104.3mg ,Sodium 225.8mg ,Carbohydrates 77.3g ,Protein 18.4g

**INGREDIENTS**

- 2 C. fine semolina

- 1 C. plain flour

- 1 pinch salt

- 1 C. whole wheat flour

- 1 C. warm water

- 3 eggs

- 2 C. milk

- 2 tsp. baking powder

- 1 tbsp. vegetable oil

- 1 tbsp. instant yeast

- 2 tsp. sugar

**DIRECTIONS**

**Step 1**

Get a large mixing bowl: Mix in it the semolina with flours, baking powder, yeast, sugar, and salt.

**Step 2**

Mix in the milk with water. Combine them well until you get a thick batter.

**Step 3**

Place a skillet over medium heat. Pour in it a ladle of the batter in a circle shape.

**Step 4**

Let it cook until dries out and have holes all over it without flipping it.

**Step 5**

Slide it to a serving plate that is covered with a kitchen towel.

**Step 6**

Repeat the process with the remaining batter.

**Step 7**

Serve you crepes hot with some butter and honey, jam or chocolate syrup.

**Step 8**

Enjoy.

# ALGERIAN MASH FOR TOAST

**Prep Time:** 10 mins

**Total Time:** 30 mins

**Servings per Recipe:** 6

## NUTRITIONAL VALUE

Calories 43.0 ,Fat 0.4g ,Cholesterol 0.0mg ,Sodium 4.3mg ,Carbohydrates 10.0g ,Protein 1.7g

## INGREDIENTS

- 2 eggplants,1/2 inch slices
- 2 garlic cloves, crushed
- 1 tsp. sweet paprika
- 1 1/2 tsp. cumin, ground
- 1/2 tsp. sugar
- 1 tbsp. lemon juice

## DIRECTIONS

**Step 1**

Season the eggplant slices with some salt. Place them in a sieve and let them sit for 32 min.

**Step 2**

Once the time is up, rinse them and dry them.

**Step 3**

Place a large skillet over medium heat. Heat in it 1/4 inch of oil.

**Step 4**

Cook in it the eggplant slices until they become golden brown.

**Step 5**

Drain them and place them on some paper towels to cool down for few minutes.

**Step 6**

Finely chop them and place them in a sieve to drain for 5 min.

**Step 7**

Get a large mixing bowl: Combine in it the chopped eggplant with cumin, sugar, and paprika.

**Step 8**

Stir them to coat. Pour the mixture into a hot pan and cook them for 2 to 3 min.

**Step 9**

Stir in the lemon juice with a pinch of salt then serve it hot.

**Step 10**

Enjoy.

# MEDITERRANEAN LAMB STEW

**Prep Time:** 25 mins

**Total Time:** 55 mins

**Servings per Recipe:** 6

**NUTRITIONAL VALUE**

Calories 547.7 ,Fat 31.6g ,Cholesterol 191.2mg ,Sodium 152.5mg ,Carbohydrates 5.5g ,Protein 58.1g

**INGREDIENTS**

- 1/4 C. vegetable oil

- 1 1/2 lbs. cubed lamb stew meat

- 1/2 C. chopped parsley

- 1 1/2 tsp saffron

- 1 tbsp butter

- salt

- 1 lemon, cut into wedges

- pepper

- 1 large onion, chopped

- 1 C. water

**DIRECTIONS**

**Step 1**

Place a large pan over medium heat. Heat in the oil. Brown in it the lamb pieces for 4 min on each side.

**Step 2**

Sprinkle over it the saffron, a pinch of salt and pepper.

**Step 3**

Stir in the onion with water. Cook them until they start boiling. Lower the heat and put on the lid.

**Step 4**

Let them cook for 16 min over low heat. Remove the lid and add the butter.

**Step 5**

Let them cook for 8 min.

**Step 6**

Garnish your stew the parsley and lemon wedges. Serve it warm.

**Step 7**

Enjoy.

# NORTH AFRICAN FRITTATAS

**Prep Time:** 15 mins

**Total Time:** 1 hr 25 mins

**Servings per Recipe:** 6

## NUTRITIONAL VALUE

Calories 230.6 ,Fat 15.0g ,Cholesterol 268.8mg ,Sodium 360.9mg ,Carbohydrates 8.8g ,Protein 15.5g

## INGREDIENTS

- 1 eggplant

- 1/4 tsp ground pepper

- 1 tbsp extra virgin olive oil

- 1/8 tsp ground cinnamon

- 1 medium onion, chopped

- 1 tsp harissa, dissolved in 1 tbsp of water

- 1 medium red bell pepper, diced

- 1/4 lb. gruyere cheese, grated

- 8 large eggs

- 1/2 bunch flat leaf parsley, minced

- 2 garlic cloves, minced

- 1/4 tsp rose water

- 1/2 tsp salt

## DIRECTIONS

### Step 1

Before you do anything, preheat the oven to 450 F.

### Step 2

Use a sharp knife to make slits in the eggplant without cutting it all the way through.

**Step 3**

Place it on a baking sheet and coat it with olive oil.

**Step 4**

Roast it in the oven for 22 min. Decrease the oven temperature to 350 min.

**Step 5**

Place the eggplant aside to lose heat for 10 min. Peel it and dice it.

**Step 6**

Place a pan over medium heat. Heat in it 1 tbsp of olive oil.

**Step 7**

Cook in it the bell pepper with onion for 9 min. Stir in the garlic with eggplant, and a pinch of salt.

**Step 8**

Cook them for an extra 2 min. parsley, rose water, salt, pepper, cinnamon, and harissa.

**Step 9**

Fold the eggplant mixture into the eggs with cheese. Pour the mixture in a greased baking pan.

**Step 10**

Cook it in the oven for 32 min. Allow your omelet to rest for 12 min then serve it.

**Step 11**

Enjoy.

# HARISSA AND EGGS SKILLET

**Prep Time:** 5 mins

**Total Time:** 40 mins

**Servings per Recipe:** 4

**NUTRITIONAL VALUE**

Calories 426.8 ,Fat 37.2g ,Cholesterol 372.0mg ,Sodium 861.3mg ,Carbohydrates 10.4g ,Protein 14.7g

**INGREDIENTS**

- 2 sweet green bell peppers, deseeded

- 2 chili peppers, deseeded

- 1 tbsp caraway seed

- 2 fluid oz. tomato paste

- 1 tsp salt

- 24 fluid oz. water

- 1/2 tsp black pepper

- 4 fluid oz. extra virgin olive oil

- 8 large eggs

- 1 tbsp paprika

- 2 tbsp harissa

**DIRECTIONS**

**Step 1**

Get a blender: Place in it the chilies with bell pepper. Blend them smooth.

**Step 2**

Place a skillet over medium heat. Heat in it the oil.

**Step 3**

Stir in the pepper mixture with tomato paste, harissa, caraway seeds, tomato paste, salt, and pepper.

**Step 4**

Stir in the water and cook them until they start boiling. Lower the heat and let them cook for 22 min.

**Step 5**

Spread the sauce in the pan then crack the eggs on top. Put on the lid and let them cook for 16 min over low heat.

**Step 6**

Serve your eggs skillet warm with some bread.

**Step 7**

Enjoy.

# ALGERIAN CHICKEN THIGHS AND LEGS

**Prep Time:** 20 mins

**Total Time:** 1 hr 40 mins

**Servings per Recipe:** 4

**NUTRITIONAL VALUE**

Calories 397.5 ,Fat 27.6g ,Cholesterol 81.7mg ,Sodium 2496.8mg ,Carbohydrates 16.3g ,Protein 23.3g

**INGREDIENTS**

- 1 tbsp. kosher salt

- 4 medium yellow onions, cut into 12 wedges

- 6 garlic cloves, roughly chopped

- each

- 2 tsp. cumin seeds, crushed

- fresh ground black pepper, to taste

- 2 tsp. paprika

- 1 lemon, thinly sliced crosswise seeds removed 1 tsp. ground turmeric

- 1 1/4 C. green olives, pitted

- 5 tbsp. olive oil

- 1/3 C. fresh cilantro, minced

- 4 skinless chicken thighs

- hot cooked rice

- 4 skinless chicken drumsticks

- 1 tsp. saffron thread, crushed

## DIRECTIONS

### Step 1

Get a mortar: Mash in it the garlic with salt using a pestle until they become like a paste.

### Step 2

Pour them into a mixing bowl and add the cumin, paprika, and turmeric. Add 3 tbsp. of oil and mix them well.

### Step 3

Stir in the chicken thighs and drumsticks. Cover them with a cling foil.

### Step 4

Let it sit for 4 to 5 min the fridge.

### Step 5

Place a large pot over high heat. Heat in it the rest of the oil until it starts shimmering.

### Step 6

Fry in it the chicken thighs and drumsticks until they become golden brown.

### Step 7

Drain them and place them on paper towels to drain.

**Step 8**

Stir the onion with saffron, a pinch of salt and pepper into the pot.

**Step 9**

Cook them for 16 min while stirring. Add the chicken thighs and drumsticks back with lemon slices and 1 C. water.

**Step 10**

Cook them until they start boiling. Lower the heat and put on the lid.

**Step 11**

Cook them for 40 to 42 until the chicken is done.

**Step 12**

Stir in the olives with cilantro. Adjust the seasoning of your stew then serve it hot.

**Step 13**

Enjoy.

# NORTH AFRICAN VEGETABLE SOUP

**Prep Time:** 20 mins

**Total Time:** 55 mins

**Servings per Recipe:** 4

**NUTRITIONAL VALUE**

Calories 138.6 ,Fat 3.9g ,Cholesterol 0.0mg ,Sodium 434.6mg ,Carbohydrates 23.7g ,Protein 3.5g

**INGREDIENTS**

- 1 onion

- 2 garlic cloves

- 1 C. garbanzo beans
- 2 tbsp. cilantro
- 2 tbsp. bulghur wheat
- 2 tbsp. olive oil
- 8 C. water
- 2 carrots, large pieces
- 1 tsp. salt
- 1 large potato, large pieces
- pepper, to taste
- 1 1/2 C. butternut squash, large pieces
- 1 tsp. paprika
- 2 tbsp. tomato paste
- 1 pinch cayenne

## DIRECTIONS

**Step 1**

Place a large skillet over medium heat. Heat in it the oil.

**Step 2**

Cook in it the garlic with onion for 3 min. Stir in the cilantro with seasonings and veggies.

**Step 3**

Stir in the water and put on the lid. Cook them for 16 min.

**Step 4**

Once the time is up, drain the veggies and mash them. Stir them back into the pot.

**Step 5**

Stir in the tomato paste, garbanzos, and bulghur wheat.

**Step 6**

Cook them for 12 to 16 min. Adjust the seasoning of your stew then serve it hot.

**Step 7**

Enjoy.

# NAAN ALGERIA

**Prep Time:** 50 mins

**Total Time:** 54 mins

**Servings per Recipe:** 1

**NUTRITIONAL VALUE**

Calories 183.4 ,Fat 9.8g ,Cholesterol 0.0mg ,Sodium 195.9mg ,Carbohydrates 21.8g ,Protein 4.0g

**INGREDIENTS**

- 3 C. finely ground whole wheat flour

- 1 tsp. salt

- 1/2 C. olive oil, divided

- 1 1/2 C. water

- 1 tsp. ground cumin

- 1 tsp. sweet paprika

- 1 tsp. turmeric

**DIRECTIONS**

**Step 1**

To prepare the dough:

**Step 2**

Get a mixing bowl: Combine in it the flour with salt and 2 tbsp. of oil.

**Step 3**

Add the water gradually while mixing until you get smooth dough.

**Step 4**

Transfer it t a lightly floured working surface and knead it for 14 min.

**Step 5**

Grease a large bowl with 2 tbsp. of oil. Shape the dough into a ball and place it in it.

**Step 6**

Cover it with a cling foil and let it rest for 60 min.

**Step 7**

Get a mixing bowl: Whisk in it the cumin, paprika, turmeric, and remaining 1/4 C. oil.

**Step 8**

To prepare the flatbread:

**Step 9**

Shape the dough into 12 balls. Layover them a cling foil to cover them.

**Step 10**

Place a dough ball on a lightly floured surface. Roll it into a disk until it becomes thin.

**Step 11**

Place a griddle over medium heat. Cook in it the bread until it becomes puffy and golden brown on both sides.

**Step 12**

Repeat the process with the remaining dough.

**Step 13**

Serve your bread warm or cold with some stew, honey, butter, or olive oil.

**Step 14**

Enjoy.

# POMEGRANATES AND ORANGES

**Prep Time:** 30 mins

**Total Time:** 40 mins

**Servings per Recipe:** 4

**NUTRITIONAL VALUE**

Calories 263.0 ,Fat 0.3g ,Cholesterol 0.0mg ,Sodium 5.6mg ,Carbohydrates 67.0g ,Protein 1.4g

**INGREDIENTS**

- 1 1/2 C. water
- 1 C. sugar
- 1/4 C. thinly sliced peeled ginger
- 4 green cardamom pods
- 3 whole star anise
- 6 any small oranges
- 1/2 C. pomegranate seeds

**DIRECTIONS**

**Step 1**

Place a large saucepan over medium heat.

**Step 2**

Stir in it the water, sugar, ginger, cardamom, and star anise. Cook them until they start boiling.

**Step 3**

Lower the heat and cook them for 10 to 12 min while stirring often.

**Step 4**

Turn off the heat and put on the lid. Cook them for 16 min until the mixture becomes syrupy.

**Step 5**

Strain it and place it in the fridge to lose heat completely for at least 120 min.

**Step 6**

Peel the oranges and slice them into segments. Transfer them to a serving bowl and add to them the syrup.

**Step 7**

Let them sit for 60 min with the lid on in the fridge.

**Step 8**

Garnish them with pomegranate seeds then serve it.

**Step 9**

Enjoy.

# SEMOLINA BREAD WITH CHILI SPREAD

**Prep Time:** 20 mins

**Total Time:** 40 mins

**Servings per Recipe:** 6

**NUTRITIONAL VALUE**

Calories 799.2 ,Fat 26.6g ,Cholesterol 0.0mg ,Sodium 591.8mg ,Carbohydrates 118.2g ,Protein 20.7g

**INGREDIENTS**

- Bread

- 4 vine ripened tomatoes

- 2 lbs. semolina, medium ground

- 1 tbsp. olive oil

- 1 1/2 tsp. salt

- 5 garlic cloves, minced

- 3 C. water

- 1 green chili pepper

- 4 tbsp. olive oil

- salt

- 6 tbsp. olive oil, for frying

- Spread/Dip

- 2 large red bell peppers

**DIRECTIONS**

**Step 1**

To prepare the pepper dip/spread:

**Step 2**

Before you do anything, preheat the oven broiler.

**Step 3**

Place the bell peppers with tomatoes on a baking sheet.

**Step 4**

Broil them in the oven for 8 min while flipping them every 2 to 3 min.

**Step 5**

Allow them to cool down completely then peel them and discard the seeds.

**Step 6**

Place a large skillet. Heat in it 1 tbsp. of olive oil. Cook in it the garlic with chili for 1 min.

**Step 7**

Drain them and transfer them to a food processor. Add to them the roasted tomatoes and bell peppers.

**Step 8**

Pulse them several times until they become finely chopped.

**Step 9**

Pour the mixture into a bowl and place it in the fridge until ready to serve.

**Step 10**

To prepare the bread:

**Step 11**

Get a large mixing bowl: Mix in it the semolina with 4 tbsp. of olive oil and salt.

**Step 12**

Add the water gradually while mixing until you get smooth elastic dough.

**Step 13**

Shape it into 6 balls then roll them until they become 1/4 inch thick.

**Step 14**

Place a large pan over medium heat. Heat in it 1 tbsp. of olive oil.

**Step 15**

Cook in it the dough circles for 3 to 5 min on each side until they become golden brown.

**Step 16**

Enjoy.

# ALGERIAN FRIES

**Prep Time:** 20 mins

**Total Time:** 1 hr 10 mins

**Servings per Recipe:** 6

**NUTRITIONAL VALUE**

Calories 332.8 ,Fat 13.5g ,Cholesterol 53.9mg ,Sodium 962.1mg ,Carbohydrates 41.6g ,Protein 12.2g

**INGREDIENTS**

- 2 tbsp. oil

- 1/2 C. onion, chopped

- 1/2 tsp. cinnamon

- 1 lb. skinless chicken piece

- 3 C. water

- 10 sprigs flat leaf parsley, leaves only,

- 2 lbs. frozen French fries

- chopped

- 1 egg, beaten

- 1/4 C. chickpeas, cooked

- lemon wedge

- 1 tsp. black pepper

- 1 tsp. salt

**DIRECTIONS**

**Step 1**

Place a large skillet over medium heat. Heat in it the 2 tbsp. of oil.

**Step 2**

Stir in it the onion, chicken, 1/2 the parsley, chickpeas, pepper, salt and cinnamon.

**Step 3**

Put on the lid and cook them for 10 to 12 min. Stir in the water and cook them until they start boiling.

**Step 4**

Prepare the French fries by following the instructions on the package.

**Step 5**

Stir the beaten egg with fries into the pot and cook them for 10 to 12 min.

**Step 6**

Garnish it with parsley then serve it hot.

**Step 7**

Enjoy.

# LEILA'S DESSERT (PUDDING)

**Prep Time:** 15 mins

**Total Time:** 50 mins

**Servings per Recipe:** 6

**NUTRITIONAL VALUE**

Calories 519.5 ,Fat 23.9g ,Cholesterol 0.0mg ,Sodium 118.3mg ,Carbohydrates 72.5g ,Protein 12.1g

**INGREDIENTS**

- 1/2 lb. dates, pitted and finely chopped

- 1 C. sugar

- 1 C. almonds, blanched & chopped

- 1 C. unsalted dry roasted peanuts

- 4 egg whites, stiffly beaten

**DIRECTIONS**

**Step 1**

Before you do anything, preheat the oven to 325 F.

**Step 2**

Get a mixing bowl: Combine in it the dates, sugar, almonds, and peanuts.

**Step 3**

Add the egg whites and combine them well. Pour the mixture into a greased baking pan.

**Step 4**

Bake it for 36 to 42 min. Serve it hot with extra toppings of your choice.

**Step 5**

Enjoy.

# BALSAMIC BEETS

**Prep Time:** 10 mins

**Total Time:** 1 hr 10 mins

**Servings per Recipe:** 4

**NUTRITIONAL VALUE**

Calories 87.2 ,Fat 6.8g ,Cholesterol 0.0mg ,Sodium 38.6mg ,Carbohydrates 6.5g ,Protein 0.8g

**INGREDIENTS**

- 4-6 beetroots

- 1-2 tsp sugar

- 1-2 tbsp balsamic vinegar

- 1/2 lemon, juice

- 2 tbsp olive oil

- salt

- 1 bunch mint leaves, sliced

## DIRECTIONS

### Step 1

Bring a large saucepan of water to a boil. Cook in it the beetroots until they become soft.

### Step 2

Drain them and dice them. sugar, balsamic vinegar, lemon juice, olive oil, and a pinch of salt.

### Step 3

Stir in the diced beets with mint. Chill your salad in the fridge until ready to serve.

### Step 4

Enjoy.

# MARIAM'S SALAD

**Prep Time:** 10 mins

**Total Time:** 20 mins

**Servings per Recipe:** 6

## NUTRITIONAL VALUE

Calories 178.3 ,Fat 14.9g ,Cholesterol 62.1mg ,Sodium 140.3mg ,Carbohydrates 8.6g ,Protein 3.0g

## INGREDIENTS

- 1 lb. carrot, peeled and sliced

- 1/4 tsp harissa

- 3 tbsp flat leaf parsley, minced

- 12 black olives

- 1 tsp cumin, ground

- 2 hard-boiled eggs, quartered

- 1/3 C. olive oil

- 1/4 C. red wine vinegar

- 2 garlic cloves

**DIRECTIONS**

**Step 1**

Place a large saucepan over medium heat. Bring in it 2 C. of water to a boil.

**Step 2**

Stir in the carrots with a pinch of salt. Cook them until they become soft then drain them.

**Step 3**

Get a mixing bowl: Whisk in it the parsley, cumin, olive oil, vinegar, garlic, harissa, salt, and pepper.

**Step 4**

Add the carrots with eggs, and olives. Toss them to coat.

**Step 5**

Chill the salad in the fridge for about 30 min then serve it.

**Step 6**

Enjoy.

# SPICY PAN-FRIED BEEF

**Prep Time:** 10 mins

**Total Time:** 25 mins

**Servings per Recipe:** 4

**NUTRITIONAL VALUE**

Calories 64.8 ,Fat 7.0g ,Cholesterol 0.0mg ,Sodium 12.2mg ,Carbohydrates 0.8g ,Protein 0.2g

**INGREDIENTS**

- 4 (6 oz.) filet of beef
- 1 tsp coriander seed, crushed
- 1/2 tsp white peppercorns, crushed
- 1 tsp dried ancho chile powder
- 1 tsp ground cumin
- 2 tbsp olive oil
- salt

**DIRECTIONS**

**Step 1**

Place a large pan over medium heat. Heat in it the oil.

**Step 2**

Get a mixing bowl: Stir in it the coriander, peppercorns, chili powder and cumin.

**Step 3**

Massage the mixture into the beef fillets. Season them with some salt and pepper.

**Step 4**

Place them in the hot pan and cook them for 5 to 7 min on each side until they are done. Serve them warm.

**Step 5**

Enjoy.

# HOT CHICKPEA SALAD

**Prep Time:** 15 mins

**Total Time:** 35 mins

**Servings per Recipe:** 6

**NUTRITIONAL VALUE**

Calories 226.2 ,Fat 6.1g ,Cholesterol 0.0mg ,Sodium 543.2mg ,Carbohydrates 39.9g ,Protein 6.2g

**INGREDIENTS**

- 1 1/2 lbs. carrots, quartered and sliced
- 1/2 tsp ground cumin
- 2 tbsp golden raisins
- 1/2 tsp salt
- 2 tbsp canola oil
- 19 oz. chickpeas, drained and rinsed
- 2 onions, sliced
- 1 pinch cayenne pepper
- 1/2 tsp hot red pepper flakes
- 1 lemon
- 1/2 tsp caraway seed
- 1/2 tsp paprika

**DIRECTIONS**

**Step 1**

Place a large salted saucepan of water to a boil. Cook in it the carrots until they become soft.

**Step 2**

Drain them and place them aside to cool down for a while. Place 1/2 C. of the cooking water aside.

**Step 3**

Get a mixing bowl: Place in it the raisins and cover them with hot water. Let them sit for 12 min then drain them.

**Step 4**

Place a skillet over medium heat. Heat in it the oil. Cook in it the onion for 12 min.

**Step 5**

Stir in the raisins with carrot water, red pepper flakes, caraway seeds, cumin, paprika, and a pinch of salt.

**Step 6**

Cook them until they start boiling. Stir in the carrot slices and let them cook for 5 min.

**Step 7**

Add the chickpeas with a pinch of cayenne pepper. Cook them for 3 min.

**Step 8**

Serve your chickpeas salad warm with some lemon wedges.

**Step 9**

Enjoy.

# POTATO SALAD IN NORTH AFRICA

**Prep Time:** 15 mins

**Total Time:** 30 mins

**Servings per Recipe:** 4

**NUTRITIONAL VALUE**

Calories 208.2 ,Fat 7.5g ,Cholesterol 1.9mg ,Sodium 18.9mg ,Carbohydrates 32.6g ,Protein 4.3g

**INGREDIENTS**

- 1 1/2 lbs. potatoes
- 1/4 tsp harissa, see appendix
- 1 tsp ground cumin
- 1 large lemon, juice
- 2 tbsp extra virgin olive oil
- 1/4 C. plain yogurt
- 2 tbsp cilantro, minced

**DIRECTIONS**

**Step 1**

Bring a large salted saucepan of water to a boil. Cook in it the potatoes until they become soft.

**Step 2**

Drain them, peel them and dice them.

**Step 3**

Get a mixing bowl: Mix in it the harissa with lemon juice, cumin, oil, yogurt, and cilantro.

**Step 4**

Add the potatoes with a pinch of salt and pepper. Toss them to coat.

**Step 5**

Serve your salad chilled or warm.

**Step 6**

Enjoy.

# GINGER SHRIMP

**Prep Time:** 15 mins

**Total Time:** 20 mins

**Servings per Recipe:** 4

**NUTRITIONAL VALUE**

Calories 240.0 ,Fat 14.9g ,Cholesterol 220.8mg ,Sodium 258.8mg ,Carbohydrates 1.5g ,Protein 24.1g

**INGREDIENTS**

- 1 lb. unshelled shrimp, peeled
- 1 bunch cilantro, chopped
- 2 garlic cloves, chopped
- salt and pepper
- 4 tbsp olive oil
- lemon wedge
- 1 tsp cumin
- 1/2 tsp ground ginger
- 1 tsp paprika
- 1/4 tsp cayenne

**DIRECTIONS**

**Step 1**

Before you do anything, preheat the oven broiler.

**Step 2**

Use a knife to cut a slit in the middle of the shrimp in the shape of a butterfly.

**Step 3**

Get a mixing bowl: Whisk in it the oil with garlic, cumin, ginger, paprika, cayenne, cilantro, a pinch of salt and pepper.

**Step 4**

Place the shrimp on a baking tray. Drizzle over them the oil mixture and toss them to coat.

**Step 5**

Cook the shrimp in the oven broiler for 5 min. Serve them warm with some lemon.

**Step 6**

Enjoy.

# NORTH AFRICAN FLORETS

**Prep Time:** 5 mins

**Total Time:** 25 mins

**Servings per Recipe:** 4

**NUTRITIONAL VALUE**

Calories 171.1 ,Fat 13.8g ,Cholesterol 0.0mg ,Sodium 628.3mg ,Carbohydrates 11.0g ,Protein 3.6g

**INGREDIENTS**

- 8 oz. tomatoes, chopped

- 2 large garlic cloves, finely chopped

- 4 tbsp. olive oil

- 1 tsp. paprika

- 1 tsp. salt

- 1 tsp. black pepper

- 1 tsp. harissa

- 1 cauliflower, medium-sized, trimmed, cut

- into florets

**DIRECTIONS**

**Step 1**

Bring a large salted pot of water to a boil. Cook in it the cauliflower for 8 min.

**Step 2**

Place a small pan over medium heat. Heat in it the oil. Cook in it the garlic 1 min.

**Step 3**

Stir in the tomatoes, salt, pepper, paprika, and harissa. Lower the heat and cook them for 10 to 12 min.

**Step 4**

Once the time is up, drain the cauliflower and add it to the pan.

**Step 5**

Toss them to coat and serve them hot.

**Step 6**

Enjoy.

# HOW TO MAKE HARISSA

**Prep Time:** 40 mins

**Total Time:** 40 mins

**Servings per Recipe:** 8

**NUTRITIONAL VALUE**

Calories 73.4 ,Fat 2.7g ,Cholesterol 0.0mg ,Sodium 451.1mg ,Carbohydrates 12.5g ,Protein 2.0g

**INGREDIENTS**

- 4.5 oz. dried hot red chili peppers, seeded
- 1 1/2 tsps salt
- and stemmed
- 1 tsp water
- 1/2 head garlic
- 1-3 tbsp olive oil
- 1 1/2 tsps caraway seeds
- 1 1/2 tsps ground coriander

**DIRECTIONS**

**Step 1**

Get a bowl: Place in it the chili peppers and cover them with hot water. Let them sit for 30 min.

**Step 2**

Strain them and transfer them to a food processor.

**Step 3**

Add the garlic with the remaining ingredients. Blend them smooth.

**Step 4**

Adjust the seasoning of your harissa then serve it.

**Step 5**

Enjoy.

# SMOKED CHILI HARISSA

**Prep Time:** 25 mins

**Total Time:** 35 mins

**Servings per Recipe:** 1

**NUTRITIONAL VALUE**

Calories 1115.6 ,Fat 111.4g ,Cholesterol 0.0mg ,Sodium 1200.5mg ,Carbohydrates 32.2g ,Protein 7.2g

**INGREDIENTS**

- 4 smoked chili peppers, seeded
- 8 dried hot red chili peppers
- 1 tbsp cumin seed
- 2 tsp coriander seeds
- 1 tsp caraway seed
- 8 garlic cloves
- 1/2 C. olive oil
- 1/2 tsp salt

**DIRECTIONS**

**Step 1**

Place the chili peppers in a bowl. Cover them with hot water. Let them sit for 25 min then drain them.

**Step 2**

Place a pan over medium heat. Cook in it the cumin, coriander, and caraway seeds 2 min.

**Step 3**

Get a food processor: Place in it the toasted seeds with chilies, garlic, olive oil, and salt.

**Step 4**

Process them until they become smooth. Spoon the mixture into an airtight container.

**Step 5**

Store it in the fridge for up to 60 days.

**Step 6**

Enjoy.

# NORTH AFRICAN SPICE MIX

**Prep Time:** 10 mins

**Total Time:** 10 mins

**Servings per Recipe:** 1

**NUTRITIONAL VALUE**

Calories 19.1 ,Fat  0.6 g ,Cholesterol  0.0 mg ,Sodium  583.9 mg ,Carbohydrates 3.8 g ,Protein  0.4 g

**INGREDIENTS**

- 2 tsp ground nutmeg

- 1 1/2 tsp sugar

- 2 tsp ground coriander

- 1 1/2 tsp paprika

- 2 tsp ground cumin

- 1 1/2 tsp ground black pepper

- 2 tsp ground ginger

- 1 tsp cayenne pepper

- 2 tsp turmeric

- 1 tsp cardamom powder

- 2 tsp salt

- 1 tsp ground allspice

- 2 tsp cinnamon

- 1/2 tsp ground cloves

## DIRECTIONS

### Step 1

In a bowl, add all the ingredients and mix well.

### Step 2

Transfer the mixture into a glass jar and seal tightly.

### Step 3

Store in a cool, dry place.

# POTATO SOUP IN ALGERIA

**Prep Time:** 15 mins

**Total Time:** 55 mins

**Servings per Recipe:** 6

## NUTRITIONAL VALUE

Calories 31.5 ,Fat 2.3g ,Cholesterol 3.2mg ,Sodium 150.0mg ,Carbohydrates 1.0g ,Protein 1.6g

## INGREDIENTS

- 2 1/4 lb. fish fillet, cubed

- 1 tbsp. cumin

- 2 large potatoes, diced

- 1 tsp. ras el hanout, see appendix

- 2 green bell peppers, diced

- 1 tsp. coriander

- 1 large carrot, diced

- 2 bay leaves

- 1 fennel bulb, diced

- 1 piece lemon rind

- 2 onions, diced

- 1 tbsp. harissa

- 1 celery rib, diced

- 4 tbsp. olive oil

- 4 tbsp. tomato paste

- 8 1/2 C. water or vegetable broth

**DIRECTIONS**

**Step 1**

Place a large soup pot over medium heat. Heat in it the oil.

**Step 2**

Cook in it the onion for 3 min. Stir in the bell peppers, potatoes, carrot, fennel, and celery.

**Step 3**

Cook them for 3 to 5 min. Stir in the tomato paste and cook them for 30 sec.

**Step 4**

Stir in the water with bay leaves, seasonings, and lemon rind.

**Step 5**

Bring them to a simmer then lower the heat and cook them for 22 min.

**Step 6**

Stir in the fish and cook them for an extra 16 min.

**Step 7**

Adjust the seasoning of your soup then serve it hot as it is or blend it smooth.

**Step 8**

Enjoy.

# ALGERIAN LAMB SHOULDER

**Prep Time:** 20 mins

**Total Time:** 1 hr 40 mins

**Servings per Recipe:** 4

**NUTRITIONAL VALUE**

Calories 787.1 ,Fat 59.5g ,Cholesterol 163.3mg ,Sodium 744.0mg ,Carbohydrates 22.1g ,Protein 42.3g

**INGREDIENTS**

- 3 tbsp oil

- 2 lbs boneless lamb shoulder, 1-inch chunks

- 1/2 tsp. saffron or 1/2 tsp. turmeric

- 1 medium onion, chopped

- 4 C. water

- 4 garlic cloves, minced

- 1 1/2 lbs green beans, 2-inch pieces

- 1 tsp. salt

- 2 tomatoes, diced

- 1/4 tsp. fresh ground black pepper

- 1 medium onion, sliced in rings

- 1 tsp. ground cumin

- 4 tbsp parsley, chopped

- 1/2 tsp. cayenne pepper

- 1 tsp. ground cumin

## DIRECTIONS

### Step 1

Place a pot over medium heat. Heat in it the oil.

### Step 2

Cook in it the lamb with garlic and onion for 5 min.

### Step 3

Stir in the salt, pepper, 1 tsp. cumin, cayenne, and saffron. Cook them for 2 min.

### Step 4

Stir in the tomato with water. Heat them until they start boiling. Lower the heat and put on the lid.

### Step 5

Cook them for 46 min. Stir in the green beans and cook them for 10 to 12 min.

### Step 6

Sir in the onion with parsley and 1 tsp. of cumin. Cook them for an extra 10 to 12 min.

### Step 7

Adjust the seasoning of your stew then serve it hot with some couscous.

### Step 8

Enjoy.

# LAMB TAGINE WITH SAFFRON

**Prep Time:** 20 mins

**Total Time:** 3 hr 20 mins

**Servings per Recipe:** 4

**NUTRITIONAL VALUE**

Calories 933.8 ,Fat 40.6g ,Cholesterol 120.0mg ,Sodium 923.9mg ,Carbohydrates 89.4g ,Protein 62.1g

**INGREDIENTS**

- 2 lbs. lamb, cut into pieces
- 3 tbsps olive oil
- 3 lbs. artichokes
- 1 preserved lemon
- 3 lbs. green peas
- 1/2 lb. olive, green
- 1 tsp ginger
- 1 bunch parsley
- 1 pinch saffron
- lemon juice
- 1 clove garlic

**DIRECTIONS**

**Step 1**

Get a large mixing bowl: Mix in it the olive oil with garlic, ginger, and saffron.

**Step 2**

Add the lamb pieces and toss them to coat.

**Step 3**

Place a tagine or stew pot over medium heat. Heat in it 1 tbsp of olive oil.

**Step 4**

Brown in it the meat pieces for 3 to 4 min on each side.

**Step 5**

Arrange the artichoke hearts on top followed by the olives, preserved lemon, 1/2 C. of water, a pinch of salt and pepper.

**Step 6**

Put on the lid and let it cook over the lowest heat setting for 1 h 30 min to 2 h until the meat is done.

**Step 7**

Serve your lamb tagine warm with some bread.

**Step 8**

Enjoy.

# ARABIAN MEATBALL SOUP

**Prep Time:** 20 mins

**Total Time:** 2 hr 5 mins

**Servings per Recipe:** 6

**NUTRITIONAL VALUE**

Calories 707.9 ,Fat 55.9g ,Cholesterol 140.6mg ,Sodium 1959.0mg ,Carbohydrates 18.0g ,Protein 33.0g

**INGREDIENTS**

- Meat

- 2 tbsps olive oil

- Stew

- 1 small yellow onion, minced

- 1/4 C. olive oil

- 1 lb. ground chuck

- 1 lb. beef short rib

- 1 tbsp ground cumin

- kosher salt & ground black pepper

- 1 tbsp ground black pepper

- 4 garlic cloves, chopped

- 1 tbsp cilantro, minced

- 1 large yellow onion, minced

- 1 tbsp parsley, minced

- 5 C. beef stock

- 2 1/4 tsps kosher salt

- 6 oz. spinach leaves, chopped

- 1 1/2 tsps paprika

- 1 (16 oz.) cans white kidney beans, rinsed

- 3/4 tsp ground cinnamon

- drained

- 1 egg, beaten

- cooked couscous

**DIRECTIONS**

**Step 1**

To prepare the meatballs:

**Step 2**

Place a soup pot over high heat. Heat in it 1 tbsp of oil.

**Step 3**

Cook in it the onion for 6 min. Transfer it to a mixing bowl with the chuck, cumin, pepper, cilantro, parsley, salt, paprika, cinnamon, and egg. Shape the mixture into meatballs.

**Step 4**

Heat another tbsp of oil in the saucepan. Brown in it the meatballs for 5 min. Drain them and place them aside.

**Step 5**

To prepare the soup:

**Step 6**

Sprinkle some salt and pepper all over the ribs. Brown them for 7 min. Drain them and place them aside.

**Step 7**

Stir the onion with garlic into the saucepan. Let them cook for 6 min.

**Step 8**

Add the ribs back with stock. Cook them until they start boiling. Lower the heat and let them cook for 60 min.

**Step 9**

Stir in the meatballs and let them cook for an extra 9 min. Stir in the beans with spinach for 5 min.

**Step 10**

Adjust the seasoning of your ribs and meatballs stew. Serve it hot.

**Step 11**

Enjoy.

# TUNA GYROS

**Prep Time:** 10 mins

**Total Time:** 10 mins

**Servings per Recipe:** 4

**NUTRITIONAL VALUE**

Calories 260.3 ,Fat 8.8g ,Cholesterol 109.4mg ,Sodium 644.4mg ,Carbohydrates 26.9g ,Protein 17.7g

**INGREDIENTS**

- 1/8 cayenne pepper

- 1/2 C. roasted red pepper, chopped

- 2 tbsps lemon juice

- 2 tbsps drained capers

- 1 tbsp olive oil

- 24 inches pita bread, split open

- 2 hard-boiled eggs, peeled and chopped

- 2 C. packed arugula, chopped

- 1 (6 oz.) cans tuna, drained

- 1 C. halved cherry tomatoes

**DIRECTIONS**

**Step 1**

Get a mixing bowl: Toss in it the spices, eggs, tuna, tomato, olive oil, roasted pepper, capers, and arugula.

**Step 2**

Season them with some salt. Spoon the salad into pita wraps then serve them.

**Step 3**

Enjoy.

*

# 26ALGERIAN LEG OF LAMB

**Prep Time:** 10 mins

**Total Time:** 2 hr 10 mins

**Servings per Recipe:** 4

**NUTRITIONAL VALUE**

Calories 235.8 ,Fat 11.9g ,Cholesterol 0.0mg ,Sodium 828.4mg ,Carbohydrates 28.8g ,Protein 6.4g

**INGREDIENTS**

- 4 pieces leg of lamb

- 4 carrots, peeled, chunked

- 1 tsp. curry powder

- 4 yellow zucchini, chunked

- 1 tsp. cumin

- 1 C. chickpeas, soaked overnight

- 1 tsp. ground coriander

- 1 medium onion, diced

- 4 C. water or broth

- 1 tsp. salt

- 3 tbsp. oil

- 1 tsp. ras el hanout, see appendix

**DIRECTIONS**

**Step 1**

Place a large soup pot over medium heat. Heat in it the oil.

**Step 2**

Cook in it the meat with onion for 4 min. Stir in the water with seasonings and chickpeas.

**Step 3**

Lower the heat and put on the lid. Cook them for 60 min.

**Step 4**

Once the time is up, stir in the veggies and put on half a cover.

**Step 5**

Cook them for 60 min until the veggies are done.

**Step 6**

Adjust the seasoning of you stew then serve it hot.

**Step 7**

Enjoy.

# WHOLE CHICKEN

**Prep Time:** 15 mins

**Total Time:** 55 mins

Mediterranean Style **Servings per Recipe:** 4

**NUTRITIONAL VALUE**

Calories 356.3 ,Fat 23.4g ,Cholesterol 100.3mg ,Sodium 1393.7mg ,Carbohydrates 13.3g ,Protein 24.0g

**INGREDIENTS**

- 1 chicken, cut-up
- 1/4 tsp. thyme
- 2 tsp. salt
- 1 tbsp. parsley, minced
- 1/4 tsp. pepper
- 2 tbsp. butter
- 1/2 C. chicken broth
- 1 garlic clove, crushed
- 1 medium eggplant, pared and diced
- 1 medium onion, chopped
- 2 fresh tomatoes, peeled and chopped

**DIRECTIONS**

**Step 1**

Coat the chicken with paprika, 1 tsp. of salt and pepper.

**Step 2**

Place a large pan over medium heat. Heat in it the butter until it melts.

**Step 3**

Cook in it the chicken pieces for 3 to 4 min on each side. Drain them and place them aside.

**Step 4**

Pour the broth into the pan. Stir in the garlic, eggplant, onion, and tomatoes; sprinkle with remaining salt, thyme, and parsley.

**Step 5**

Heat them until they start boiling. Stir in the chicken and put on the lid.

**Step 6**

Cook them for 32 min over low heat until it the chicken done. Serve it warm.

**Step 7**

Enjoy.

# MINT AND TOMATO LENTILS WITH LAMB

**Prep Time:** 15 mins

**Total Time:** 1 hr 5 mins

**Servings per Recipe:** 4

**NUTRITIONAL VALUE**

Calories 368.4 ,Fat 1.1g ,Cholesterol 0.0mg ,Sodium 185.0mg ,Carbohydrates 64.4g ,Protein 25.9g

**INGREDIENTS**

- 2 C. green lentils, soaked overnight and
- drained
- 1 tsp. ras el hanout
- 1 onion, finely chopped
- olive oil, to fry
- 3 garlic cloves, minced
- 2 pints water
- 1 carrot, grated
- 1 lamb stock cube or 1 beef stock cube
- 1 courgette, grated

- salt & pepper

- 1 tsp. dried mint

- 4 pieces lamb or 4 pieces chicken

- 1/2 tsp. tomato puree

**DIRECTIONS**

**Step 1**

Place a pan over medium heat. Heat in it a splash of oil.

**Step 2**

Cook in it the garlic with onion for 4 min. Stir in the meat and cook them for another 4 min.

**Step 3**

Transfer the mixture to a pressure cooker. Stir in the remaining ingredients.

**Step 4**

Put on the lid and cook them for 40 to 46 min on high pressure.

**Step 5**

Adjust the seasoning of your stew then serve it hot.

**Step 6**

Enjoy.

# HOW TO MAKE FAVA BEANS

**Prep Time:** 15 mins

**Total Time:** 20 mins

**Servings per Recipe:** 4

**NUTRITIONAL VALUE**

Calories 144.9 ,Fat 5.5g ,Cholesterol 7.6mg ,Sodium 27.8mg ,Carbohydrates 17.9g ,Protein 6.8g

## INGREDIENTS

- 12 oz. frozen fava beans
- 1 tbsp butter
- 4-5 scallions, sliced
- 1 tbsp chopped cilantro
- 1 tsp chopped of mint
- 1/2-1 tsp ground cumin
- 2 tsps olive oil
- salt

## DIRECTIONS

### Step 1

Bring a salted pot of water to a boil. Cook it the fava beans for 5 min until they become soft.

### Step 2

Strain them and peel them.

### Step 3

Place a skillet over medium heat. Heat in it the butter. Cook in it the fava beans with scallions for 3 min.

### Step 4

Add the cilantro with mint, cumin, olive oil and a pinch of salt. Cook them for 1 min.

### Step 5

Serve your salad right away.

### Step 6

Enjoy.

# MY FIRST TAGINE

**Prep Time:** 15 mins

**Total Time:** 2 hr 45 mins

**Servings per Recipe:** 4

**NUTRITIONAL VALUE**

Calories 279.1 ,Fat 25.2g ,Cholesterol 0.0mg ,Sodium 83.5mg ,Carbohydrates 14.2g ,Protein 2.4g

**INGREDIENTS**

- 7 tbsp. olive oil

- 1 lemon, juice of

- 1/2 C. fresh cilantro, chopped with heavy

- 2 lbs. fish steaks diced

- stems removed

- fresh ground black pepper, to taste

- 4 garlic cloves

- 4 ripe plum tomatoes, halved lengthwise

- 3 inches gingerroot, peeled and chopped

- 1 medium onion, diced

- 2 tsp. ground cumin

- 1 red bell pepper, diced

- 1 tsp. ground coriander

- 1 green bell pepper, diced

- 1/2 tsp. anise seed

- 2 C. eggplants, diced

- 1/4 tsp. cayenne pepper

- 1/4 C. pitted black olives

- salt, to taste

- cilantro leaf, chopped

**DIRECTIONS**

**Step 1**

Get a food processor: Combine in it 4 tbsp. of olive oil with cilantro, garlic, ginger, cumin, coriander, anise, cayenne pepper, 1/4 tsp. salt and lemon juice.

**Step 2**

Blend them smooth. Pour the mixture into a large mixing bowl.

**Step 3**

Add the fish cubes and toss them to coat. Put on the lid and let them sit in the fridge for 120 min.

**Step 4**

Before you do anything else, preheat the oven to 300 F.

**Step 5**

Arrange the tomatoes in a roasting dish. Drizzle over them 1 tbsp. of olive oil with a pinch of salt.

**Step 6**

Place it in the oven and let it cook for 1 h 30 min.

**Step 7**

Drain the tomatoes and roughly chop them.

**Step 8**

Place a large pan over medium heat. Heat in it the rest of the oil.

**Step 9**

Cook in it the peppers with onion. Cook them for 6 min. Stir in the eggplant and cook them for 6 min.

**Step 10**

Stir in the olives with tomatoes, a pinch of salt and pepper.

**Step 11**

Transfer the mixture to a baking pan. Top it with the fish cubes.

**Step 12**

Put on the lid and bake it for 22 to 32 min. Serve it hot.

**Step 13**

Enjoy.

# NORTH AFRICAN HANDMADE SAUSAGE

**Prep Time:** 35 mins

**Total Time:** 35 mins

**Servings per Recipe:** 1

**NUTRITIONAL VALUE**

Calories 306.9 ,Fat 22.5g ,Cholesterol 78.1mg ,Sodium 306.6mg ,Carbohydrates 5.8g ,Protein 19.9g

**INGREDIENTS**

- 2 lbs. boneless lamb, ground

- 4 oz. lamb, fat attached to the lamb kidney

- 1 tbsp. red hot chili powder

- 2 heads garlic, peeled and minced

- 2 tbsp. sweet paprika

- 1 tsp. salt

- 1 C. cold water

- 1 tsp. black pepper

- 1 small lamb intestine casing

- 1 tbsp. ground cumin

- 1 tbsp. ground coriander

- 1 tbsp. sumac

## DIRECTIONS

### Step 1

Get a food processor: Combine in it the fat from the lamb kidney with garlic and ground lamb.

### Step 2

Pulse them several times until they become smooth.

### Step 3

Add the cumin, coriander, sumac, chili powder, paprika, salt, pepper, and water.

### Step 4

Processor them until they become smooth.

### Step 5

Spoon the mixture into the casing while twisting it after measuring 4 inches.

### Step 6

Fry them in a pan, or grill them then serve them hot.

### Step 7

Enjoy.

# PEPPER AND TOMATO BOREK

**Prep Time:** 40 mins

**Total Time:** 1 hr

**Servings per Recipe:** 10

**NUTRITIONAL VALUE**

Calories 342.0 ,Fat 3.6g ,Cholesterol 0.0mg ,Sodium 4.0mg ,Carbohydrates 66.1g ,Protein 10.2g

**INGREDIENTS**

- Filling

- Pastry

- 4 onions, sliced

- 17.5 oz. fine semolina

- 2 tbsp. concentrated tomato puree

- 9 oz. plain flour

- 2 green peppers, strips

- salt

- 2 tbsp. olive oil

- water

- salt & pepper

- 1 hot pepper

**DIRECTIONS**

**Step 1**

To prepare the filling:

**Step 2**

Place a large skillet over medium heat. Heat in it the oil.

**Step 3**

Cook in it the peppers with onion for 3 min. Stir in the tomato puree with a pinch of salt and pepper.

**Step 4**

Cook them for 6 min. turn off the heat and let the mixture cool down completely.

**Step 5**

To prepare the pastry:

**Step 6**

Combine in it the flour with semolina. Add a pinch of salt and a drizzle of olive oil. Mix them well.

**Step 7**

Add water gradually while mixing until you get stiff dough. Knead it for 10 min while adding more water until it becomes soft and elastic.

**Step 8**

Shape it into balls in the shape of a golf ball. Place one of them on an oiled working surface until it becomes thin.

**Step 9**

Put in the middle of it 2 tsp. of the filling. Pull the dough sides over the filling in the shape of a square.

**Step 10**

Place a large skillet over medium heat. Heat in it a splash of vegetable oil.

**Step 11**

Cook in it the pastry until it becomes golden brown on both sides.

**Step 12**

Repeat the process with the remaining dough and filling. Serve them warm.

**Step 13**

Enjoy.

# ALGERIAN POACHED EGGS (SHAKSHOUKA II)

**Prep Time:** 1 hr 35 mins

**Total Time:** 3 hr 35 mins

**Servings per Recipe:** 8

**NUTRITIONAL VALUE**

Calories 908.7 ,Fat 29.0g ,Cholesterol 70.3mg ,Sodium 473.1mg ,Carbohydrates 125.0g ,Protein 34.9g

**INGREDIENTS**

- 1 yellow onion, chopped

- 8 lamb chops or 8 skinless chicken pieces

- 1 C. chickpeas, drained

- 3 garlic cloves, chopped

- 2 tsp. ras el hanout spice mix

- 2 medium carrots, sliced

- salt & pepper

- 2 medium zucchini, sliced

- 1 pinch dried mint

- 2 large potatoes, diced

- 1 tbsp. sunflower oil or 1 tbsp. vegetable oil 1/4 swede or 1/4 turnip, diced

- 1 C. of liquidized tomato puree

- 1 parsnip, diced

- 6 1/2 C. water

- 1 large green chili, roughly chopped

**DIRECTIONS**

**Step 1**

Place a large skillet over medium heat. Heat in it the oil.

**Step 2**

Stir in it ras el hanout with meat. Cook them for 3 min.

**Step 3**

Stir in the zucchini, with parsnip, carrot, potato, and swede.

**Step 4**

Stir in 4 C. of water with chili pepper, a pinch of salt and pepper.

**Step 5**

Put on the lid and lower the heat. Cook it for 42 min.

**Step 6**

Stir in the chickpeas with dry mint, and 2 1/2 C. water. Cook it for an extra 32 min with the lid on.

**Step 7**

Adjust the seasoning of your soup then serve it hot.

**Step 8**

Enjoy.

# NORTH AFRICAN ORANGE GRILLED CHICKEN

**Prep Time:** 25 mins

**Total Time:** 25 mins

**Servings per Recipe:** 4

**NUTRITIONAL VALUE**

Calories 556.3 ,Fat 38.2g ,Cholesterol 150.9mg ,Sodium 143.2mg ,Carbohydrates 15.3g ,Protein 37.1g

**INGREDIENTS**

- 4 tbsp harissa

- 2 tbsp olive oil

- 16-20 chicken wings

- 4 blood oranges, quartered

- salt

- icing sugar

- cilantro, chopped

**DIRECTIONS**

**Step 1**

Before you do anything, preheat the grill and grease it.

**Step 2**

Get a mixing bowl: Whisk in it the oil with harissa.

**Step 3**

Season the chicken wings with some salt and pepper. Coat them with the oil mixture.

**Step 4**

Place them on the grill and let them cook for 6 to 9 min on each side.

**Step 5**

Coat the blood orange wedges with icing sugar. Grill them until they become charred.

**Step 6**

Serve your chicken wings next to the grilled orange wedges.

**Step 7**

Enjoy.

# GARBANZO SOUP BOWLS

**Prep Time:** 8 hr

**Total Time:** 11 hr

**Servings per Recipe:** 8

**NUTRITIONAL VALUE**

Calories 168.7 ,Fat 8.2g ,Cholesterol 23.2mg ,Sodium 100.1mg ,Carbohydrates 18.2g ,Protein 6.5g

**INGREDIENTS**

- 230 g dried garbanzo beans, soaked

- overnight

- person

- 2 C. vegetarian beef broth

- harissa, with some water

- 4 garlic cloves

- 1 pinch ground cumin

- 3 tbsp extra virgin olive oil

- ground pepper

- salt

- 16 olives

- pepper

- capers

- 8 eggs, hard-boiled and peeled

- diced roasted red pepper

- 1/2 C. day-old French bread, cubed per

- extra virgin olive oil

- 1 lemon wedge, per person

**DIRECTIONS**

**Step 1**

Before you do anything, preheat the oven to 200 F.

**Step 2**

Place an ovenproof pot over high heat. Stir in it the chickpeas with garlic, oil, stock salt, and pepper.

**Step 3**

Cover them with water. Cook them until they start boiling. Put on the lid and transfer the pot to the oven.

**Step 4**

Let them cook for 3 h.

**Step 5**

Place a slice of bread in each serving bowl. Pour over it the chickpea soup followed by the hard-boiled egg.

**Step 6**

Drizzle some harissa on top with olives, cumin, and extra toppings of your choice.

**Step 7**

Serve your soup bowl warm with some lemon wedges on the side.

**Step 8**

Enjoy.

# CAYENNE CARROT APPETIZER

**Prep Time:** 15 mins

**Total Time:** 30 mins

**Servings per Recipe:** 4

**NUTRITIONAL VALUE**

Calories 166.9 ,Fat 10.8g ,Cholesterol 0.0mg ,Sodium 121.7mg ,Carbohydrates 17.0g ,Protein 1.8g

**INGREDIENTS**

- 1 1/2 lbs. carrots, peeled, cut into rounds
- 1/2 C. water
- 3 tbsp olive oil
- 3 tbsp white vinegar
- 2 1/4 tsp ground cumin
- 1/3 C. chopped cilantro
- 1/4 tsp cayenne pepper

**DIRECTIONS**

**Step 1**

Bring a salted saucepan of water to a boil. Cook in it the carrots until they become soft. Drain them.

**Step 2**

Place a large pan over medium heat. Heat in it the oil. Cook in it the cayenne pepper with cumin for 20 sec.

**Step 3**

Stir in the carrots with water and vinegar. Cook them for 4 min.

**Step 4**

Adjust the seasoning of your salad then stir in the cilantro. Serve it warm.

**Step 5**

Enjoy.

# ALGERIAN GLAZED ROUNDED FLATBREAD

**Prep Time:** 20 mins

**Total Time:** 1 hr 15 mins

**Servings per Recipe:** 15

**NUTRITIONAL VALUE**

Calories 348.8 ,Fat 18.8g ,Cholesterol 101.0mg ,Sodium 194.5mg ,Carbohydrates 43.2g ,Protein 4.3g

**INGREDIENTS**

- Flatbread

- 1 C. egg

- Syrup

- 1 C. sugar

- 2 C. granulated sugar

- 1 C. butter or 1 C. margarine

- 4 C. water

- 1 C. of freshly ground almonds

- 1 1/2 tbsp. orange blossom water

- 1 C. stale bread

- 1 1/2 tsp. baking powder

- 1 lemon, zest of, large

- 1/2 tsp. vanilla essence

## DIRECTIONS

### Step 1

Before you do anything, preheat the oven to 350 F

### Step 2

To prepare the syrup:

### Step 3

Place a heavy saucepan over medium heat. Combine in it the water with sugar.

### Step 4

Heat in it until it starts boiling. Stir in the blossom water and cook them for 2 min.

### Step 5

Turn off the heat and let the syrup cool down completely.

### Step 6

To prepare the bread:

### Step 7

Get a large mixing bowl: Cream in it the eggs in until they become pale.

**Step 8**

Add the sugar with butter and beat them until they become smooth **Step 9**

Stir in the bread with almonds, lemon zest, and vanilla extract.

**Step 10**

Pour the batter into a greased baking pan. Bake it for 42 min until it becomes golden.

**Step 11**

Once the time is up, pour the syrup over the hot bread. Let it sit in the turned off oven for 6 min.

**Step 12**

Once the time is up, serve it warm with toppings of your choice.

**Step 13**

Enjoy.